Lost!

Jacqueline Martin

Name _____

Age _____

Class _____

OXFORD
UNIVERSITY PRESS

OXFORD
UNIVERSITY PRESS

Great Clarendon Street, Oxford OX2 6DP

Oxford University Press is a department of the University of Oxford.
It furthers the University's objective of excellence in research, scholarship,
and education by publishing worldwide in

Oxford New York

Auckland Cape Town Dar es Salaam Hong Kong Karachi
Kuala Lumpur Madrid Melbourne Mexico City Nairobi
New Delhi Shanghai Taipei Toronto

With offices in

Argentina Austria Brazil Chile Czech Republic France Greece
Guatemala Hungary Italy Japan South Korea Poland Portugal
Singapore Switzerland Thailand Turkey Ukraine Vietnam

OXFORD and OXFORD ENGLISH are registered trade marks of
Oxford University Press in the UK and in certain other countries

ISBN-13: 978 0 19 440093 0

Printed in China

Illustrations by: Garry Davies

With thanks to Sally Spray for her contribution to this series

Reading Dolphins
Notes for teachers & parents

📖 Using the book

1 Begin by looking at the first story page (page 2). Look at the picture and ask questions about it. Then read the story text under the picture with your students. **Use section 1 of the CD for this if possible.**

2 Teach and check the understanding of any new vocabulary. Note that some of the words are in the **Picture Dictionary** at the back of the book.

3 Now look at the activities on the right-hand page. Show the example to the students and instruct them to complete the activities. This may be done individually, in pairs, or as a class.

4 Do the same for the remaining pages of the book.

5 Retell the whole story more quickly, reinforcing the new vocabulary. **Sections 2 and 3 of the CD can help with this.**

6 **If possible, listen to the expanded story (section 4 of the CD). The students should follow in their books.**

7 When the book is finished, use the **Picture Dictionary** to check that students understand and remember new vocabulary. **Section 5 of the CD can help with this.**

💿 Using the CD

The CD contains five sections.

1 The story told slowly, with pauses. Use this during the first reading. It may also be used for "Listen and repeat" activities at any point.

2 The story told at normal speed. This should be used once the students have read the book for the first time.

3 The story chanted. Students may want to chant along with the story.

4 The expanded story. The story is told in a longer version. This will help the students understand English when it is spoken faster, as they will now know the story and the vocabulary.

5 Vocabulary. Each word in the **Picture Dictionary** is spoken and then used in a simple sentence.

Come on, James. Let's go to the store.

Can I buy some candy, please?

OK.

Circle yes or no .

1. James is a boy.

(yes)
no

2. James is with his mom.

yes
no

3. James has a red shirt.

yes
no

4. James has the keys.

yes
no

5. James is going to the store.

yes
no

6. James is going to school.

yes
no

7. James wants some candy.

yes
no

8. It's a hot day.

yes
no

We need to buy apples, bananas, bread, eggs, juice, milk, and rice. James, can you get the milk and juice, please?

Write.

1 I like to eat  <u>bread</u> .

2 I like to drink _____ .

3  _____ is good for you.

4  _____ is white.

5  _____ come from a hen.

6  _____ grow on trees.

7  _____ are yellow.

Juice and milk.
Oh, look. What is that?
It is a balloon! I want it.

Find and write.

① Rich wants apples_____.

② Jill wants _____.

③ Tina wants _____.

④ Greg wants _____.

Oh, no! Where is James?

Who is James?

He is my son. He has black hair.

Write and connect.

a<u>pples</u>   •

b_____   •

m_____   •

e_____   •

r_____   •

f_____   •

o_____   •

j_____   •

b_____   •

1

2

3

4

5 MILK

6

7

8 BREAD

9

Oh, no! I cannot get it.
Where is Mom? Where am I?
I am lost.

Circle yes **or** no .

❶ James is in the supermarket.

yes
(no)

❷ The balloon is blue.

yes
no

❸ James is lost.

yes
no

❹ James has the balloon.

yes
no

❺ James is with his mom.

yes
no

❻ Can you see cars in
the street?

yes
no

❼ Can you see trees in
the street?

yes
no

Hello.

Hello, what's wrong?

I cannot find my mommy.

Trace and count.

pencils ⟦7⟧ crayons ⟦ ⟧

rulers ⟦ ⟧ erasers ⟦ ⟧

pens ⟦ ⟧ notebooks ⟦ ⟧

Oh dear! Don't worry.
Come on.
Let's go to the police station.

Rearrange the words.

❶ lost is James.

<u>James is lost.</u>

❷ old years is He seven.

_____

❸ cannot mother He find his.

_____

❹ in shop He a is.

_____

❺ woman James helps A.

_____

Good morning. What's the matter?

I'm lost. I cannot find my mommy.

What can you see on page 16?
Circle yes or no .

1 Is there a ruler? yes / no

2 Is there a girl? yes / no

3 Is there a pen? yes / no

4 Is there a sandwich? yes / no

5 Is there a notebook? yes / no

6 Is there a phone? yes / no

7 Is there a police officer? yes / no

8 Is there an eraser? yes / no

What is your name?

James Lee.

How old are you?

I am seven years old.

Circle.

1. James ⟨**is**⟩ / am seven years old.

2. James is a girl / **boy** .

3. James is on / **in** the police station.

4. The police officer **is** / are asking questions.

5. James is happy / **lost** .

6. The woman is looking **at** / in James.

7. James is asking / **answering** questions.

8. James **can** / cannot find his mother.

What is your telephone number, James?

It is 357642.

Let's call your mother. Three, five, seven, six, four, two.

Rearrange the words.

1 Lee His is James name.

His name is James Lee.

2 a has James shirt red.

_____

3 police station the James in is.

_____

4 357642 is telephone number His.

_____

5 wants go James home to.

_____

James! Are you OK?

Yes, mommy. I am not lost.

Thank you so much!

You're welcome!

Write. Tell the story.

❶ James and his m<u>other</u> go
to the supermarket.

❷ James sees a yellow b_____ .

❸ James w_____ the balloon.

❹ James gets l_____ .

❺ James goes into a s_____ .

❻ James goes to the police
s_____ .

❼ Mom says t_____ you.

Picture Dictionary

apple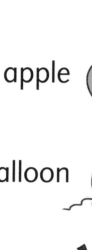

egg

balloon

eraser

banana

fish

bread

hair

candy

hen

crayon

juice

milk

police officer

notebook

rice

orange

ruler

pen

sandwich

pencil

tree

phone

Dolphin Readers

Dolphin Readers are available at five levels, from Starter to 4.

The Dolphins series covers four major themes:

Grammar, Living Together, The World Around Us, Science and Nature.

For each theme, there are two titles at every level.

Activity Books are available for all Dolphins.

All Dolphins are available on audio CD.
(2 TITLES ON EACH CD ⬤ SEE TABLE BELOW)

Teacher's Notes are available at **www.oup.com/elt/dolphins**

	Grammar	Living Together	The World Around Us	Science and Nature
Starter	• Silly Squirrel • Monkeying Around	• My Family • A Day with Baby	• Doctor, Doctor • Moving House	• A Game of Shapes • Baby Animals
Level 1	• Meet Molly • Where Is It?	• Little Helpers • Jack the Hero	• On Safari • Lost Kitten	• Number Magic • How's the Weather?
Level 2	• Double Trouble • Super Sam	• Candy for Breakfast • Lost!	• A Visit to the City • Matt's Mistake	• Numbers, Numbers Everywhere • Circles and Squares
Level 3	• Students in Space • What Did You Do Yesterday?	• New Girl in School • Uncle Jerry's Great Idea	• Just Like Mine • Wonderful Wild Animals	• Things That Fly • Let's Go to the Rainforest
Level 4	• The Tough Task • Yesterday, Today and Tomorrow	• We Won the Cup • Up and Down	• Where People Live • City Girl, Country Boy	• In the Ocean • Go, Gorillas, Go